DK Life Stories

Leonardo da ViNci

DK Life Stories

Leonardo da ViNci

by Stephen Krensky

Illustrated by Charlotte Ager

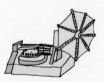

Senior Editors Marie Greenwood, Roohi Sehgal
Designer Charlotte Jennings

Editors Steve Setford, Abhijit Dutta
Art Editor Mohd Zishan
Jacket Coordinator Issy Walsh
Jacket Designer Dheeraj Arora
DTP Designers Vikram Singh, Sachin Gupta
Picture Researcher Rituraj Singh
Assistant Pre-Producer Abi Maxwell
Senior Producer Amy Knight
Managing Editors Laura Gilbert,
Monica Saigal, Jonathan Melmoth
Deputy Managing Art Editor Ivy Sengupta
Managing Art Editor Diane Peyton Jones
Delhi Team Head Malavika Talukder
Creative Director Helen Senior
Publishing Director Sarah Larter

Art History Consultant Leslie Primo
Literacy Consultant Stephanie Laird

First American Edition, 2020
Published in the United States by DK Publishing
1450 Broadway, Suite 801, New York, NY 10018

Copyright © 2020 Dorling Kindersley Limited
DK, a Division of Penguin Random House LLC
20 21 22 23 24 10 9 8 7 6 5 4 3 2 1
001–316567–Feb/2020

A catalog record for this book is available from the Library of Congress.
ISBN: 978-1-4654-9064-3 (Paperback)
ISBN: 978-1-4654-9065-0 (Hardcover)

DK books are available at special discounts when purchased in bulk for sales promotions,
premiums, fund-raising, or educational use. For details, contact:
DK Publishing Special Markets, 1450 Broadway, Suite 801, New York, NY 10018
SpecialSales@dk.com

Printed and bound in China

A WORLD OF IDEAS:
SEE ALL THERE IS TO KNOW

www.dk.com

Dear Reader,

It's hard to put a single label on Leonardo da Vinci: painter, sculptor, engineer, architect, philosopher— he was all of these things. Yet even when taken together, it is possible that something is still missing. Maybe it's simply the genius that allowed him to master so many professions at once.

Leonardo lived in an age of political, economic, and cultural upheaval, but he tried to sidestep the turbulence of his times to focus on his art. "The evil that does not harm me," he wrote, most likely referring to his even temperament, "is as the good that does not help me." As famous as Leonardo became for the works he completed, he was almost as well-known for the projects that he either abandoned, left unfinished, or never found time to fully explore.

More than anything, Leonardo wanted to pursue his dreams and follow his curiosities—wherever they might lead him. The fact that he was able to do that over so much of his life may have meant more to him than the towering achievements that have endured in his name.

Stephen Krensky

The life of...
Leonardo
da Vinci

A blank **canvas**

On April 15, 1452, a baby boy was born in the Italian village of Anchiano. The exact time, his grandfather noted, was 10:30 in the evening.

The baby didn't know the village name, of course, or that Anchiano was a day's ride from the much bigger city of Florence. For that matter, he didn't know that Florence was in Italy, either.

In fact, Italy wasn't even a country in 1452. It was a collection of independent city-states. Places such as Florence, Venice, and Milan each had their own governments and ways of doing things. Sometimes they were friendly with each other, but not always.

The house in Anchiano where Leonardo was born

The city-states weren't all getting along when the baby, who was named Leonardo, came into the world. Milan and Venice were fighting, but luckily the war wasn't in Anchiano. So Leonardo, surrounded by peaceful vineyards and olive groves, was happily unaware of it.

Still, the life that lay before him was going to be challenging. His father was Ser Piero da Vinci. The title "Ser" meant that Piero was a respected gentleman. Ser Piero was a notary, a public official who helped people create legal documents and contracts. Leonardo's mother, Caterina, had no such status. She was a peasant. This wouldn't have mattered if she and Ser Piero were married, but they weren't. Therefore, any child they had was illegitimate and not protected by the law. That meant Ser Piero could have simply ignored the boy, which would have made life very difficult for Leonardo.

But Ser Piero didn't ignore his illegitimate child. He acknowledged that Leonardo was his son. However, he did not agree to marry Caterina (he was already planning to marry another young woman) or agree to take the baby into his home. So Leonardo lived with his mother for his first five years. She soon married Antonio Buti, a local furnace worker who produced lime for making pottery. Caterina and Antonio quickly started their own family, giving Leonardo several half sisters.

WHAT IS ILLEGITIMATE?

This means not recognized as lawful. In medieval Italy (and in many other places), an illegitimate child did not have the same protection under the law as a child born to a married father and mother. Under the rules of the time, illegitimate children had fewer rights than children that were born as part of a legal family. For example, they could not go to college or become a doctor or a lawyer. As an illegitimate son, Leonardo's future career choices would have been limited, hemmed in on many sides.

The children grew up to the rhythms of farm life—plowing, planting, and harvesting. As a boy, Leonardo would have learned how to look after farm animals and about olives, the most important local crop. Olives were a popular food and the oil that came from pressing them was used for cooking. Olive oil had other uses too, such as keeping machines running smoothly and being burned as a fuel in lamps.

Olives

Leonardo's earliest memory, though, concerned an incident that took place while he was still in the cradle. As Leonardo remembered it many years later, a large bird of prey—most likely a vulture—landed next to him. This in itself was not so remarkable, but what happened next was very strange indeed. The vulture opened Leonardo's lips with its feathers, then used its tail to strike him several times inside the mouth.

Why did the vulture do such a thing? Leonardo had no idea, and of course the vulture couldn't explain its actions. So the whole episode remained a mystery.

Nobody knows if this really happened or not, but Leonardo himself believed that it did. Certainly, it would have been an odd tale to make up. In any case, it was the beginning of his lifelong fascination with birds.

Later, Leonardo told stories that may well have been inspired by the everyday things around him. He once wrote a fable, for example, that told of a majestic cedar tree. This tree was so proud of its own beauty that it would not allow any lowly plants to grow near its trunk. That was all very well, until a strong wind came along. With no other plants to protect it, the tree was torn out of the ground and toppled over.

Even as a little boy, Leonardo may have understood that pride and arrogance were not qualities he wanted to adopt. Going forward, he would try to keep that in mind. But right now, his life was like a blank canvas, just waiting to be painted.

2

Moving AND monsters

Leonardo grew up in a time of great learning and discovery across western Europe. This period became known as the Renaissance.

Renaissance means "rebirth." Before this, the last 900 years (a period of time called the Dark Ages) had seen little progress, but during the Renaissance everything changed. Huge advances were made across different areas of civilization—including science, medicine, literature, and art.

DID YOU KNOW?

The Peace of Lodi lasted for 40 years, until Italy was invaded by the French, setting off a fresh round of disputes.

In Italy, the pace of change quickened once the disputes between the different city-states had ended. A treaty known as the Peace of Lodi was signed in 1454, when Leonardo was two years old.

THE RENAISSANCE

The Renaissance was a period in European history that started around 1300 and lasted about 300 years. An explosion of developments took place in literature, science, and art, especially painting and sculpture. One of the most important developments was the invention of the printing press in around 1440, which allowed the spread of knowledge through printed books. Other significant inventions of the Renaissance included the mechanical clock, eyeglasses, the telescope, and the microscope. All of them contributed to the great progress of the time.

Primavera (Spring), by the Renaissance artist Sandro Botticelli, painted around 1480

For a time, the city-states of Italy were at peace. This allowed people to concentrate on more productive pursuits than fighting. Peace left everyone feeling better—and it was no doubt good for Ser Piero's business, too.

Ser Piero now turned his attention to Leonardo, who moved from his mother's home to his father's nearby estate. Most probably Leonardo moved because he was now old enough to begin a more formal education. Unlike his mother, Leonardo's father could afford to pay for proper teaching. Here, Leonardo would spend the rest of his childhood with other members of his father's family, including his uncle and grandfather. Leonardo's new stepmother, Albiera, could have made life difficult for him, because he was not one of her own children, but she didn't. Albiera was kind to Leonardo and made him feel at home.

For the son of a prominent person like Ser Piero, formal education would begin with learning to read, write, and do arithmetic.

Leonardo was neither more nor less interested in his studies than most other boys of his age. His lessons were taught in common Italian, not the language of advanced education, Latin. (Leonardo learned this much later and largely on his own.)

Though Leonardo may not have been the most dedicated of students, his time away from the classroom certainly wasn't wasted. When he wasn't studying, he spent long hours wandering the countryside. He became a great collector, of rocks and flowers and bits of wood—anything unusual that caught his attention.

One of the few known stories from Leonardo's childhood tells of a hike he took in the countryside. He came across the entrance to a cave and was terrified at what might be inside. He was afraid there might be a hideous monster, and he wondered what the monster might do if it caught him. Clearly, it would be better not to find out!

At the same time, the dark opening was intriguing. What secrets did it hold? What might he discover if only he was bold enough to investigate?

Leonardo's curiosity proved stronger than his fear. Plucking up courage, he ventured cautiously inside.

Luckily, there was no monster in the cave. Instead, Leonardo's curiosity was rewarded when he came across the fossil remains of a whale embedded in the rock. How had it gotten there, so far from the ocean? Leonardo had no idea,

but to him this was a treasure as great and as valuable as a chest of gold coins. He was very happy to have found it.

Years later, Leonardo drew sketches of these walls, as he did of other memories from his childhood. Very likely many other images of animals and the countryside that later appeared in Leonardo's work were imprinted on his brain during these early years. Even as a boy, Leonardo was interested in drawing, and no doubt his artistic talent was

Fossil of an early sea mollusk

what is a fossil?

The remains or an impression of a prehistoric animal or plant preserved in rock. The whale fossil Leonardo found was millions of years old.

noticeable to anyone who saw the pictures he produced. But this ability would not flourish by itself. It required the proper direction and training. As Leonardo later wrote in his notebooks, it is not enough for an artist simply to copy what is placed in front of him. Knowledge and thought concerning what is being drawn are also needed.

"The painter who draws merely by practice and by eye, without any reason, is like a mirror which copies everything placed in front of it without being conscious of their existence."

Leonardo, from his private notebooks

Chapter 3

The young **apprentice**

**As art and culture flourished in Italy,
it became an important gateway between
much of Europe and the Far East.**

The tremendous trade in silks, spices, and other
goods from Asia that passed through Italy was
very profitable for the city-states. It made a lot
of money for a lot of people.

Some of that money was used to support
artists. Wealthy lords and merchants, known as
patrons, hired the best painters and sculptors.
The most successful and famous artists had

Travelers on trade
routes across Asia
often moved in large
caravans for safety.

large studios or workshops. There they did their own projects and also supervised the work of their apprentices. These were young students who had agreed to serve an established artist, called a master, so they could learn new skills.

Andrea del Verrocchio

Of course, not just anyone could become an artist's apprentice. A would-be apprentice needed to show enough talent to persuade a master to take him on. By now, Leonardo had been drawing for years, and his potential had convinced his father, Ser Piero, to see what could be arranged for his son.

One of these masters, the artist Andrea del Verrocchio, lived in Florence. At this time, it was necessary for craftsmen to master a range of crafts to be assured of constant work. Verrocchio was no exception and had many different skills—painting, sculpting, and working with precious metals, such as gold and silver.

In 1466, Verrocchio accepted 14-year-old Leonardo as an apprentice on a seven-year contract. Apprentices started out doing everything from sweeping the floor to mixing paints and preparing canvases. They were allowed to practice painting on tablets made from a hard wood called boxwood. The paint could be scraped off so the tablet could be reused. A story passed down by Giorgio Vasari (an Italian painter, architect, and writer) told how Ser Piero was once asked if he could have a piece of wood painted to turn it into an attractive shield. Piero agreed and brought the wood to Leonardo to see what he might do with it.

Recognizing that the shield was a weapon for battle, Leonardo decided to paint a fearsome image that would frighten anyone with the misfortune to see it.

In the end, wrote Vasari, Leonardo painted "a great animal so horrible and fearful that it seemed to poison the air with its fiery breath, with venom issuing from its open jaws, fire from its eyes, and smoke from its nostrils."

But was it really scary enough? Leonardo wanted to make sure. One morning, he placed the shield on an easel by the window, so that a shaft of soft light fell on the painting. When his father first saw it, he was startled, thinking it was not just a painting, but rather a truly terrifying beast. This pleased Leonardo, who told his father to take the painted shield, since "the work answers the purpose for which it was made."

Eventually, if his talents progressed well, an apprentice might be considered skilled enough to actually help paint some parts of his master's canvas. However, a master

DID YOU KNOW?

The shield was later sold to the Duke of Milan, who kept it safely away from any battle and admired it as a work of art.

commonly took all the credit for anything produced in his studio, even if it was largely the work of his apprentices.

The earliest picture credited to Leonardo is a pen-and-ink drawing of the Arno River flowing through a rural landscape. It shows Leonardo's growing understanding of perspective. His crosshatched lines are thicker and heavier in the foreground and lighter in the background, creating a sense of distance and depth.

Arno Valley Landscape, drawn by Leonardo in 1473

Unlike many apprentices, the ever-curious Leonardo was interested in lots of subjects beside art. They included chemistry, mechanics, engineering, and carpentry, to name just a few.

PERSPECTIVE

An artist can use perspective to create a sense of depth on a flat surface, such as in a painting or drawing. The artist makes it appear that some objects are nearby, while others lie in the distance. Artists base their paintings around simple lines to help them show perspective.

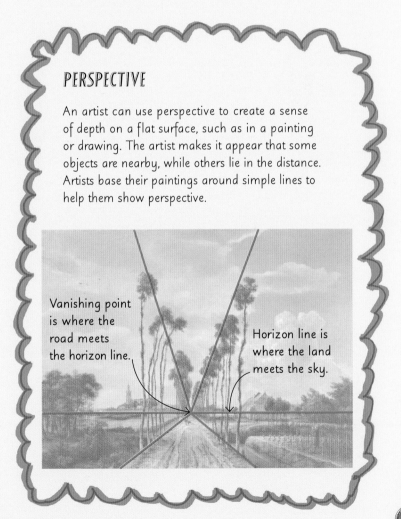

Vanishing point is where the road meets the horizon line.

Horizon line is where the land meets the sky.

He believed that the world was like a fabric woven from many threads of knowledge, and he  wanted to understand them all.

Leonardo was unique in the way he used scientific and mathematical principles to guide his work. For example, he divided the face into seven parts to help him draw it more accurately. As he wrote later, "The space between the parting of the lips and the base of the nose is one-seventh of the face."

One of Verrocchio's paintings from around 1475, *The Baptism of Christ*, has an angel on the far left that many experts believe, after studying the brushstrokes, is actually the work of Leonardo. It is the most realistic of the figures in the painting. Clearly, Leonardo was becoming ready to be a master himself.

The Baptism of
Christ by Verrocchio,
painted around 1475

29

Chapter 4

Spreading HIS wings

Having completed his apprenticeship with Verrocchio, Leonardo now set out to make a name for himself in the world of art.

Fortunately, Leonardo's father had lots of influential connections and was able to help him get commissions in Florence. So Leonardo began to meet clients and pursue his career. He dedicated himself to his work and produced everything from portrait-sized paintings and sculptures to huge wall paintings called murals.

Like other young artists, Leonardo had little time or money to promote himself. He needed to concentrate on his art, hoping that whatever he produced would put him in demand. But how long would it take to establish himself? That was impossible to say.

At least Leonardo was in the right place to make that happen. Florence was one of the major cities of western Europe.

In the 1470s, the city was a bustling place of over 40,000 people. Its rulers were the Medicis,

The city of Florence is home to many fine Renaissance buildings.

31

COSIMO DE MEDICI

Cosimo de Medici (1389–1464) oversaw the rise of the Medici family. His father had created the family's first bank, and under Cosimo it became more profitable and influential. He used his money to gain support from politicians for his various business projects. He also began the family tradition of giving financial help to artists. Having established the Medicis firmly in control of Florentine affairs, Cosimo paved the way for his descendants to rule Florence for many years after his death.

a family of bankers who rapidly increased trade and made the city incredibly wealthy. There were many rich people, who were able to sponsor talented artists.

So what did Leonardo, the budding artist, do next? Unfortunately, there is little record of his professional life in the first few years after his apprenticeship. Certainly, he was not invisible—he was known around town for his confident manner. He was also considered a good singer and musician. And it was hard to miss this handsome young man who favored colorful clothing and spent his free time walking the streets of Florence. If Leonardo was at all troubled by his lack of work or frustrated by the absence of progress in his career, he was very good at hiding it.

Sometimes, while he was out and about, Leonardo would buy a caged bird that was being offered for sale. His intention was not to take the bird home to enjoy its company. Rather, he would simply open the cage and let the imprisoned bird fly away.

Leonardo was also known for following

people—particularly anyone that he felt had an unusual feature, whether a beard or particular head of hair. Now it wasn't Leonardo's aim to make fun of whoever had caught his eye. He was just

fascinated by distinctive appearances, and he shadowed such people to give himself plenty of time to memorize their unique looks. Then Leonardo would go home and draw what he had seen.

Despite his habit of following random strangers, there was nothing random about Leonardo's approach to painting. More than most painters, he recognized a connection between science and art. For example, to be able to draw the human body properly, he knew he couldn't simply copy what he saw. He needed to understand how the body actually moved. And to properly convey light and shadow,

In this sketch from around 1480, Leonardo wanted to capture the emotions he saw in the man's face.

Using only a few pen strokes, Leonardo shows a woman who is possibly either bored by her surroundings or who feels superior to others.

This vivid drawing of a warrior's head was part of a series of sketches made by Leonardo in preparation for a large painting that he never completed.

he would have to better understand how the eye received light and formed images.

Eventually, Leonardo won the support of an important patron, Lorenzo de Medici. Lorenzo was now the leader of the ruling Medici family, although he was less interested in business dealings than his grandfather Cosimo had been. He was, however, dedicated to using his family's influence and money to encourage a flourishing culture for artists in Florence.

Lorenzo de Medici

In 1481, Leonardo received an important commission. It came from the monks in a local monastery, and its subject was a scene from the New Testament of the Bible. The title of the painting, which measured 8 ft by 8 ft (2.5 m by 2.5 m), was the *Adoration of the Magi*. The painting captured the moment when the Three Kings, or Magi, who had come from far away bearing gifts, first saw the baby Jesus.

Leonardo's unfinished painting *Adoration of the Magi*, begun in 1481

37

Securing this commission was a big step for Leonardo, but he never finished the painting. Leaving work unfinished was to become a habit throughout his life. Leonardo may not have had a short attention span, but he was certainly easily interrupted. So when he received an offer to embark on a different project, one that involved moving to nearby Milan, he jumped at the chance of a new adventure.

"Art is never finished, only abandoned."

Leonardo, from his private notebooks

Chapter 5

A change of scenery

It was hardly an accident that Leonardo ended up in Milan in 1482. He traveled to Milan at the invitation of the Sforza family.

At the time, Milan was threatened by the Papal States, which were ruled by the pope, and by Venice to the east. The Sforza family, headed by Ludovico Sforza, controlled Milan, and it needed soldiers, engineers, and other men with military experience.

Leonardo had presented himself to Ludovico as a military engineer, which was stretching the truth considering his lack of experience in battle. However, he did know a few things about the subject.

Ludovico Sforza

Leonardo's drawing of an armored tank

Leonardo had studied and drawn various kinds of war machines. While none of them had ever been built (which left open the question of whether they would actually work), his ideas were strong enough to win over Ludovico.

There was also the chance to do some sculpting. As things turned out, once Leonardo arrived in Milan, all the talk of war had calmed down, leaving him with plenty of time to work on a sculpture.

The sculpture the Sforzas had in mind was no simple

head on a pedestal. It was going to immortalize the founder of their good fortune, Francesco Sforza (1401–1466). He would be shown sitting astride a horse. The statue would be cast in bronze, stand about 16 ft (5 m) tall, and weigh around 20,000 lb (9,000 kg).

Leonardo worked steadily on the sculpture, but several years passed before he finally finished a clay model of the horse. The next step would have been to begin the casting, but the timing was unlucky. In 1499, the French invaded Milan and war broke out. The bronze earmarked for the statue was made into cannons instead.

One of Leonardo's other projects was making a silver stringed instrument in the shape of a horse's skull. This work was funded by Lorenzo de Medici. Leonardo took it with him to Milan and played it for Ludovico when his patron became the Duke of Milan in 1494. The instrument's large size and unique design gave it a rich sound, and Leonardo was able to play it with great skill.

His next undertaking, begun in 1495, was his most ambitious yet. The friars at the Church of Santa Maria delle Grazie in Milan asked Leonardo to paint a mural. Called *The Last Supper*, it was to feature Jesus and his 12 disciples (followers). The scene as described in the New Testament was the final meal they shared before one of them—Judas Iscariot—betrayed Jesus.

CHRISTIANITY

Christianity is a religion that dates from the early 1st century CE. It is based on the life and teachings of Jesus Christ, who lived in Galilee in the Middle East. Jesus's most devoted followers were called disciples. The Romans, who ruled Galilee at the time, persecuted Jesus and later crucified him, because they felt threatened by the spread of his beliefs.

Crucifixion, probably painted by Marcello Venusti in 1540

This is the *The Last Supper*, which Leonardo worked on between 1495 and 1498. Jesus is framed in the central window.

Every expression, attitude, and posture in the painting had to be examined and considered down to the smallest detail. Leonardo was very concerned to show the reactions on the disciples' faces, especially the specific expression he should give to the traitor, Judas Iscariot.

The way Leonardo worked depended on his mood. On some days, he would toil from morning till night, paintbrush in hand, never stopping even to eat or drink. On other days, he would stare at the painting for hours, thinking, but never touching the brush at all.

In fact, the prior of the church became impatient seeing Leonardo spend so much time simply staring into space lost in thought. In the prior's view, this could hardly be a good use of

what is a prior?   A prior is a Christian figure in charge of a building, such as a priory or church.

Leonardo's time—time for which the prior was paying. However, Leonardo at that point had still not decided how he should paint the faces of Jesus himself and his betrayer, Judas. When the prior

DID YOU KNOW?

It took many years to restore *The Last Supper*. The work lasted from 1978 to 1999.

hounded him for what may have seemed like one time too many, it is said that Leonardo took his revenge by painting a likeness of the prior onto the face of the traitor, Judas.

While work on *The Last Supper* progressed, Leonardo continued to follow his other interests. It is likely that Leonardo was on a steady salary, or retainer, while working for Ludovico. Leonardo drew up a new city plan for Milan, incorporating streets and canals to help people move around the city more freely. He also did smaller paintings. For though Leonardo remained in Milan for many years, his mind was constantly on the move.

47

6

The **notebooks**

Leonardo was now famous for his artistic talents and was soon to be respected for his scientific investigations.

Even so, few people knew the true extent of Leonardo's amazing ideas, because he kept most of them in a series of private notebooks.

Leonardo started to record his thoughts from a young age. The first thing he decided to do was to write everything backward from right to left. Why? It wasn't to keep his thoughts a secret. Leonardo was left-handed, and when he wrote from left to right, his hand would smear the still-wet ink as it crossed over the page. Writing from right to left overcame this problem. To most people, this approach would seem more trouble than it was worth—but not to Leonardo.

Leonardo's notebooks mixed words, drawings, geometry—whatever came into his head. Leonardo may have written his notebooks with the intention of having them published at some point.

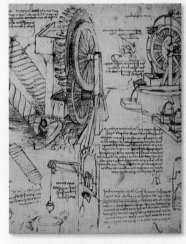

This is Leonardo's design for a "perpetual-motion" machine. The idea was that the constantly spinning wheel created energy.

He taught himself Latin, thinking that he could write up his findings. Any serious academic publication had to be written in Latin at this time, as it was the language of the educated elite.

WHAT IS MIRROR WRITING?

Mirror writing is a technique in which a person writes from right to left, instead of from left to right. For Western languages, such as Italian and English, this is the opposite of the normal way of writing. When viewed in a mirror, the reflection reverses the letters so that the text can be read in the usual way, left to right.

Art historians think that Leonardo may have written approximately 28,000 pages, filling about 50 notebooks. Around 6,500 pages survive today.

Leonardo wrote not only about painting, but also turned his attention to philosophy, the human body, architecture, warfare, and the study of plants and animals.

One of the most famous ideas in the notebooks is the Vitruvian Man. It is based on the work of the ancient Roman architect Vitruvius, who tried to find the perfect proportions in buildings and the human body. Having studied Vitruvius's writings, Leonardo set out to draw a perfectly proportioned man.

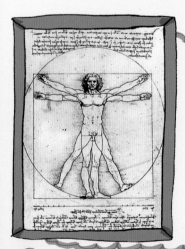

VITRUVIAN MAN

Leonardo demonstrated the ideal proportions of the body by showing an adult male with his arms and legs extended, and where his fingers and toes would touch a circle and a square that surrounded his body.

The Vitruvian Man drawn by Leonardo in his notebook in 1490

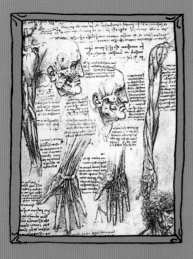

Leonardo made detailed studies of different parts of the human body. Here he has sketched arms, facial muscles, and fingers. His dissections of the human body helped him to understand it better.

With the cross-section of the eye and the human head and eye, Leonardo compared layers of the skull and brain with that of the many transparent layers of the skin of an onion.

Leonardo investigated and explored different aspects of the shoulder and neck in order to practice showing them realistically.

While the Vitruvian Man was inspired by the past, Leonardo drew many inventions that looked forward into the future. They included an underwater breathing device, a parachute, and a kind of robot— an armor-clad figure operated by gears, wheels, pulleys, and cables. Leonardo's most memorable ideas were his flying machines. He carefully studied birds and tried to understand how they fly.

FLYING MACHINES

One of Leonardo's larger flying machines was designed to carry a person lying down. The wings, made of pine and silk, would be 33 ft (10 m) across. The machine might have flown had it been somehow first carried into the air. But Leonardo never figured out how to get it off the ground.

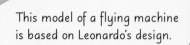

This model of a flying machine is based on Leonardo's design.

Leonardo then applied his conclusions to designs for machines.

One flying machine, called an air-screw, had a spiral blade. When turned, the blade would lift the machine into the

Reconstruction of Leonardo's design for an air-screw

air in much the same way that a modern helicopter blade lifts a helicopter. The blade, 15 ft (4.5 m) wide, would be made of linen and covered in starch to stiffen it and block pores in the fabric. Though he never built the machine, Leonardo was convinced it would have worked.

If Leonardo's ideas had been published in his lifetime, his fame would have been even greater. But he kept these ideas to himself, shut up in his notebooks, and the world ended up waiting hundreds of years until other scientists made similar discoveries for themselves.

Returning home

As an artist looking for work, Leonardo was never sure where his next job might come from. That made it hard to truly settle in one place.

But Leonardo had lots of things to think about besides which patron had money to spend or which style of art was in fashion. In this case, it was international politics that led Leonardo to leave Milan around 1500, after living there for 17 years. Earlier the Duke of Milan, worried about being attacked by Venice and Naples,

had asked the French king, King Charles VIII, for support. Charles was happy to have an excuse to invade Italy, so he agreed to step in.

But then the duke impulsively changed sides and joined with Venice and Naples against the French. Naturally, Charles didn't like that, and neither did his successor, Louis XII. When all the fighting was over, Milan was under the control of the French.

King Charles VIII

Leonardo had no particular reason to dislike the French (he really didn't concern himself much with politics), and in fact the French were interested in Leonardo's work. However, Leonardo decided it was time to leave Milan.

He made brief stays in Mantua and Venice before finally returning to Florence. He had been gone for 18 years, and the city had changed in his absence. The Medicis were no longer in power (though they were secretly plotting their return). As for the people of Florence, they

DID YOU KNOW?

One of the first things the invading French army did in Milan was use Leonardo's clay statue of a horse for target practice!

were not as cheerful as they once had been, having lived under the threat of war for years.

For the 48-year-old Leonardo, his return was more of a triumph than he might have expected. After all, few of his paintings and projects had ever been completed. So it was perhaps surprising that Leonardo enjoyed such an excellent reputation as an artist, engineer, and architect. He was liked and admired by everyone—well, almost everyone.

One notable exception was a young painter and sculptor named Michelangelo Buonarroti. No one knows exactly why the two men didn't get along with each other. Most likely, Michelangelo resented how famous Leonardo had become, despite having accomplished so little. Yes, Leonardo had ideas for paintings, but how many had he actually finished? Even *The Last Supper*, which nobody was questioning as a work of genius, had already begun to deteriorate because of the type of paints Leonardo used and the poor condition of the wall underneath.

MICHELANGELO BUONARROTI

Michelangelo Buonarroti (1475–1564) was born in Florence and was a painter, a sculptor, and an architect. Among his most famous paintings are the ones on the ceiling of the Sistine Chapel in Vatican City, Rome, where the pope lives. His sculptures include the *Pietà* (an Italian word meaning pity or compassion) and *David*. In architecture, he supervised the completion of the western end of St. Peter's Basilica—an important church in Vatican City. Michelangelo was 23 years younger than Leonardo and outlived him by 35 years, so they were only in direct competition with each other for a brief time.

Michelangelo's *Pietà*, which sits in St. Peter's Basilica, Rome, was completed in 1499, when he was only 24 years old.

In contrast, Michelangelo was a man who saw things through. When someone wanted him to carve a marble statue, the first thing he did was go to the quarry and pick out the stone himself. He took two years to sculpt the *Pietà*, an image of the Virgin Mary holding the wounded Jesus in her arms.

Later, he spent four years painting the ceiling of the Sistine Chapel in Rome—made all the more difficult by the fact he had to lie on his back while painting. Michelangelo never gave up.

Leonardo gave up all the time. Or, if he didn't actually give up, he simply became distracted and turned his attention to other things.

When he returned to Florence, his mind was focused on a new commission. He was staying as a guest at a local monastery, the Santissima Annunziata.

The monastery of Santissima Annunziata in Florence.

The monks there gave him a place to live and a workshop to paint in. Here he began working on a drawing in charcoal and black and white chalk. It was another biblical scene, this one of the Virgin Mary, the baby Jesus, St. Anne, and John the Baptist. These kinds of drawings were often called cartoons. Leonardo never went any further than the detailed drawing. However, his skill was so great that, as Vasari noted, the drawing "caused all the craftsmen to marvel."

The Virgin and Child
with St. Anne and St. John
the Baptist, drawn by
Leonardo around 1500

And when it was done,
"men and women,
young and old,
continued for two
days to flock for
a sight of it to
the room where
it was, as if to a solemn festival ..."

Michelangelo was probably not one of those patiently waiting in line to see the drawing. Even if he had been, it is unlikely that Leonardo would have noticed him—by then, Leonardo's attention would have already moved on to something else.

8

Engineering *HIS* future

Leonardo had left Milan because the French forces had arrived. Would the same army march on Florence as well?

Fortunately, after a flurry of treaties and alliances, Florence was spared from any immediate French conquest. But even with the French threat removed, the city was not safe from attack for long.

The new danger was a young military leader named Cesare Borgia. He was the illegitimate son of Pope Alexander VI, who ruled his own empire from Rome. Borgia's army was currently in northern Italy, conquering territory in his father's name.

Cesare Borgia

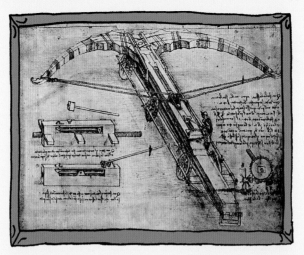

Leonardo drew a giant crossbow for use in warfare.
He sketched the mechanisms to make it work, too.

The leaders of Florence were worried that their city might be Borgia's next target. In 1502, hoping to avoid a conflict they feared they would lose, they sent two of their most respected citizens to meet Borgia and try to keep the peace.

Leonardo was one of those citizens. While he wasn't a trained negotiator, he was willing to offer his services to Borgia as a military engineer—so long as his skills were not used against Florence.

Niccolò Machiavelli

The second citizen was Niccolò Machiavelli, Florence's most talented negotiator and spy. He thought Borgia might not be as intent on conquering Florence as he appeared and could be persuaded to spare the city.

The plan worked. Borgia agreed not to attack and enlisted Leonardo's help with his military campaign. By nature, Leonardo was a peaceful man, but he was also a practical one. If working for Cesare Borgia would be both profitable and allow him to pursue his interests, then he would keep his personal views about war to himself.

In 1502, while working for Cesare Borgia, Leonardo combined his artistic and engineering skills to draw this map of the city of Imola.

So Leonardo began traveling with Borgia's army, evaluating the condition of fortresses and castles along the way. Although Borgia had no interest in Leonardo's paintings, he greatly valued another aspect of Leonardo's artistic abilities—his skill at drawing maps.

Maps were still pretty rare at the time, but an experienced commander like Cesare Borgia immediately saw how useful they could be in warfare. An army that could clearly see where it was going and what it would face in its path was an army that would be more likely to win.

Leonardo's role did not require him to do any fighting, and when the Borgia campaign ended, he was able to return to Florence in the winter of 1503. However, he was still in search of work.

Sultan Bayezid II

In one of the boldest moves of his career, he proposed some ideas to Sultan Bayezid II, who ruled the empire of the Ottoman Turks from the city of Constantinople (now called Istanbul). It had been 50 years since the Turks had taken the city away from the Byzantine Empire, which traced its roots back to the Romans. The Turks seemed busy with engineering projects, so Leonardo wrote the Sultan a letter outlining four of his ideas. The first was for a gristmill that would run on wind power rather than flowing water. The second was for a bilge pump, a machine that would remove water without using ropes or pulleys.

What is a sultan?   A sultan is a ruler in some Islamic countries.

LEONARDO'S FOUR IDEAS

In a machine called a gristmill, cereal grains, such as wheat and rye, are ground or mashed into a grainy powder that is then used to bake different kinds of bread.

A bilge pump is a kind of water pump that is used to remove excess sewage or to extract unwanted water from places such as the hull of a ship.

The main supports of a masonry bridge are made of materials, such as brick or stone, that are held together by mortar to give the bridge a secure foundation.

The deck or roadway of a suspension bridge is supported by cables that hang from towers. The towers are firmly anchored at the two ends of the bridge.

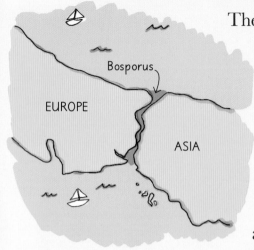

The Bosporus is a narrow stretch of water in northwestern Turkey that separates Europe and Asia.

The last two ideas were much larger projects, both for bridges. One would be a traditional masonry bridge, tall enough for ships to sail under. The other would be a true engineering marvel—a suspension bridge spanning the Bosporus. Such a bridge would have connected Europe and Asia, and Leonardo had already drawn detailed sketches to show how it could be built.

Unfortunately, Leonardo's letter went unanswered (and his ideas remained unknown until hundreds of years later). So, once again, Leonardo was faced with the challenge of figuring out what he should do next.

"Nothing can be loved or hated unless it is first understood."

Leonardo, from his private notebooks

Chapter 9

The **Mona Lisa**

**From the 1460s onward, oil paintings became
increasingly popular in Italy, and Leonardo
mainly painted in oils throughout his career.**

In the early 1500s, Leonardo was juggling several
different projects at once, including a commission
to paint a woman's portrait. Who was this woman?
Vasari was not in doubt, stating that "Leonardo
undertook to paint for Francesco del Giocondo a
portrait of Mona Lisa, his wife."

Such was Leonardo's
reputation that he could
have chosen to paint
anyone—even the
wealthiest or most
aristocratic women.
Lisa del Giocondo
was neither. So why did he agree to paint her?

WHO WAS THE MONA LISA?

Lisa Gherardini, immortalized in the *Mona Lisa*, was born in 1479. She was the oldest of seven sisters and was only 15 years old when she married Francesco del Giocondo in 1495. She was in her early 20s when Leonardo began her portrait. The name *Mona Lisa* was given to the painting by Vasari. In Italian, *mona* is a shortened form of "madonna," and is similar to politely saying "my lady" in English. For many years, the identity of the woman in the *Mona Lisa* remained open to speculation. However, in 2005, new research confirmed that Lisa del Giocondo was indeed the subject of the world's most famous painting.

Perhaps he did it as a favor to his father, who knew Lisa's husband, Francesco del Giocondo, from their business dealings. Another theory is that Lisa reminded Leonardo of his mother, and he wanted to honor her memory. Leonardo never explained his reasoning, but certainly he showed a rare dedication to the painting.

So how did Leonardo begin his most famous painting? Like many artists of his time, he chose a wood backing for smaller paintings, even though canvas was now available. To paint the *Mona Lisa*, he used poplar wood.

The choice of paint itself was also important. Many Italian painters used tempera, a water-based paint that gave a flat finish and dried quickly. Leonardo liked to use a technique called *sfumato* (from the Italian word for smoke), in which the tones and colors were gradually blended together. To achieve this effect, he needed more time for his brushstrokes than tempera allowed. Slow-drying oil paint gave him this extra time.

PAINTING TECHNIQUE

One significant aspect of Leonardo's approach to painting was his use of soft, muted colors. His images, whether of people or landscapes, never had harsh edges or bold colors that sharply contrasted with one another. Leonardo always aimed for an effect where the colors almost flowed into one another, creating a seamless whole that extended from one end of the painting to the other.

The *Mona Lisa*, which Leonardo worked on for around 16 years

"**Painting** is concerned with **all** the 10 **attributes** of sight, which are—

Darkness, Light, Solidity and **Color, Form** and **Position,** Distance and **Propinquity, Motion** and **Rest.**"

Leonardo, from his private notebooks

Several aspects of the painting were unusual. At this time, most Italian portraits were drawn from the side in profile or straight on from the front. But Leonardo painted the *Mona Lisa* as a three-quarter view from the front. He also

Profile portrait by Sandro Botticelli

set the figure against an imaginary landscape rather than against the wall of a room, which was more common. The landscape itself was noteworthy because of the amount of detail it contained. There was a winding road, some greenery, a bridge, and a river, as well as far-off icy mountains. No one place in Italy actually contained such a view, but it certainly represented aspects of the Italian countryside.

The soft curves of the background were echoed in Lisa's face and expression.

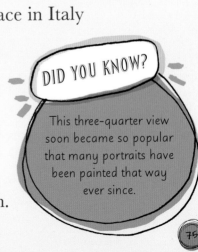

DID YOU KNOW?

This three-quarter view soon became so popular that many portraits have been painted that way ever since.

There was the hint of a smile in the line of her mouth and cheeks, but was this the beginning of a broader grin or the end of one? Leonardo never said. Many later observers thought that Lisa was pregnant, which would explain the fullness of her chin and the looseness of her clothing. Again, there was no word from Leonardo about it. According to Vasari, Leonardo chose "to have men to sing and play to her and buffoons to amuse her, to take away that look of melancholy which is so often seen in portraits."

Leonardo painting the *Mona Lisa*

Unlike many traditional portraits, which stopped just below the shoulders, Lisa's dress and hands were also included. Leonardo clearly spent long hours re-creating the folds in her clothing and ensuring that the relaxed posture of her hands matched the peaceful expression on her face.

It is likely that Leonardo began painting the *Mona Lisa* in 1503, and he continued to work at it, on and off, for many years. One of the big mysteries surrounding the portrait is why the Giocondos never received it. For all of his hard work, it seems that Leonardo never considered the portrait fully finished, so it remained in his possession for the rest of his life.

DID YOU KNOW?

The *Mona Lisa* is now in the French national art museum, the Louvre in Paris. The painting was famously stolen in 1911. It was recovered two years later.

Chapter 10

All roads LEAD TO Rome

As competing city-states, Florence and Milan often found themselves in a tug-of-war over which was the most important and powerful.

In the early 1500s, however, the two rivals found something new to compete over. That "something" was Leonardo.

Palazzo Vecchio, Florence

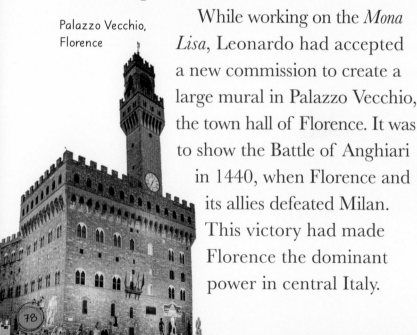

While working on the *Mona Lisa*, Leonardo had accepted a new commission to create a large mural in Palazzo Vecchio, the town hall of Florence. It was to show the Battle of Anghiari in 1440, when Florence and its allies defeated Milan. This victory had made Florence the dominant power in central Italy.

At first, Leonardo threw all his energies into the project. The sketches he did showed a group of soldiers on horseback desperately fighting for the enemy's flag, their faces reflecting the grim horrors of war. To make the moment come truly alive, Leonardo wrote in his notes of the need to show the smoke of gunfire, mixed with air and dust, which was stirred by the the movement of horses and soldiers fighting.

Flemish artist Peter Paul Rubens drew this copy of Leonardo's *Battle of Anghiari* in 1603. Leonardo's original design no longer exists.

At the same time that Leonardo received his commission for the *Battle of Anghiari*, Michelangelo was hired to paint a mural on the opposite wall to Leonardo's scene. Michelangelo's mural would commemorate the Battle of Cascina, another victory for Florence, this one over Pisa in 1364.

Whether these dueling murals would be able to happily coexist in the same room was never known, because neither painting was finished. Michelangelo completed a sketch of his composition, but he got no further than that. Leonardo, meanwhile, experimented with how best to prepare his wall for paint. He ended up with a surface that didn't hold the paint well, which halted the project.

It was around this time, in 1506, that Leonardo received an invitation to return to Milan. It was an invitation he was happy to accept, given his fond memories of having lived there for so many years.

In fact, Leonardo bounced back and forth between Milan and Florence following the death of his father, Ser Piero, in 1504. Although Leonardo was an illegitimate son, and so inherited nothing himself, he still had a duty to look after his father's estate. However, the focus

THE POPE IN ROME

In Leonardo's time, the pope lived at the Vatican in Rome, the headquarters of the Catholic Church, as he still does today. In addition to being the religious leader of the Church, the pope controlled vast areas of land in Italy, known as the Papal States. Some popes also became military leaders and tried to expand the territories they already possessed.

This portrait of a seated Pope Leo X is by Raphael. The figure on the left is Giulio di Giuliano de Medici.

of Leonardo's artistic attention remained in Milan, despite the Florentine government's attempt to lure him back to their own city.

Finally, Leonardo settled the issue of which city to stay in by choosing neither. Instead, he moved to Rome in 1513. He went there at the request of Giulio di Giuliano de Medici and his cousin, the new pope, Leo X. Both men were from the family of Leonardo's former patron, Lorenzo de Medici. Giuliano provided a handsome place where Leonardo could live and work.

The domed St. Peter's Basilica in the Vatican was being built when Leonardo arrived in Rome.

Leonardo spent much of his time in Rome carrying out scientific investigations. One important source of the Medici family's wealth at the time was making dyes to color clothing. Leonardo experimented with mirrors, trying to build a solar reflector that would focus sunlight to boil the ingredients of the dyes in less than the usual time.

Leonardo, at 61 years of age, was no longer a young man, but he could be distracted just as easily as ever. Vasari wrote that Leonardo amused himself making "little animals of a wax paste, which as he walked along he would fill with wind by blowing into them, and so make them fly in the air, until the wind being exhausted, they dropped to the ground."

Even when Leonardo's attention turned to painting, it could still be unpredictable. On one occasion when the pope entrusted him with a project, Leonardo's first step was to consider what kind of varnish he would apply to the painting after he had finished it. According to Vasari, the pope commented in some frustration that Leonardo "was a man to do nothing, for he thinks of the end before he begins his work."

Although not politically minded, Leonardo still occasionally found himself involved in delicate political situations. When the new king of France, Francis I, conquered Milan, the Medicis hoped to align themselves with the French king rather than have to fight against him. So they turned to Leonardo for help.

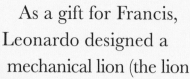

As a gift for Francis, Leonardo designed a mechanical lion (the lion was the symbol of Florence) that was able to walk for a few steps before a door opened in its chest. Tucked inside was a fleur-de-lis, the symbol of France.

The gesture may have worked even better than the Medicis had hoped. Francis was so impressed with Leonardo that he invited him to live in France. But it was an invitation, not a command. Leonardo could accept or decline it.

Leonardo pondered what to do. He realized that younger artists, such as Michelangelo and Raphael, were

What is a fleur-de-lis?

It is a stylized drawing of a lily flower that is best known as the traditional symbol of the French monarchy, when it is shown as a golden lily on a blue field. Even today, this is used as a symbol of France.

now getting more attention in Rome than he was. It must have been unsettling for Leonardo to think of himself being eclipsed by anyone else.

RAPHAEL

Along with Leonardo and Michelangelo, Raffaello Sanzio da Urbino (1483–1520), also known as Raphael, is considered one of the three greatest artists in Italy around 1500. Aside from mastering the more realistic and subtle painting techniques of the period, Raphael also distinguished his work through his bold use of color and natural composition.

Fresco, or wall painting, by Raphael, titled *The School of Athens*, painted between 1509 and 1511

While in Rome, Leonardo completed his last major painting, *St. John the Baptist*. In this striking picture, John appears to emerge from the shadows. Critics commented that he looked considerably better fed than in many other paintings. St. John was usually shown as a thin figure who, having lived in the desert, had not had the chance to eat many good meals.

Painting *St. John the Baptist* may have been a struggle for the aging Leonardo, since he now had ailments that made some of his movements difficult. But Leonardo still had enough determination and strength to accept King Francis I's invitation and manage one final move—to France.

St. John the Baptist,
Leonardo's last major
work, completed in
around 1515

Chapter 11

Final days

One thing that Leonardo may not have known about King Francis I, his new patron, was how he became king of France in the first place.

King Francis I

At his birth, Francis had been way down the line of people with a claim to the French throne. But one heir died unexpectedly, another had no children, and existing laws did not allow women with better claims to rule. So when his cousin (and father-in-law) Louis XII died, Francis, age 21, was next in line to be king.

King Francis was a great supporter of writing and the arts, which began when he invited Leonardo to France. King Francis also

standardized the French
language, eliminating
the variations that
existed in different
regions of his kingdom.

What mattered most
to Leonardo was the fact
that the king was a gracious
host. The French Court was based at Amboise in
the Loire Valley. The king lived in the Château
d'Amboise, a grand palace that had become a
favorite home of recent French kings. It had been
renovated and expanded, and now had many
more rooms than Francis needed.

Château d'Amboise,
home of Francis I.

91

Leonardo, along with his assistants and servants, took about three months to make the 900-mile (1,500-km) journey from Rome. There were no incidents reported along the way, and he was in no particular hurry. This was just as well, since he was no longer in any condition to travel fast.

Once Leonardo arrived in Amboise, he found everything to be in order. He was given his own manor, the Clos Lucé, which was connected to Château d'Amboise through an underground tunnel.

Officially, he was supposed to be painting or making engineering and architectural plans, but in truth he spent little time on these things.

Some of this inactivity may have simply been a result of his natural tendency to be easily distracted. However, historians think that he also suffered a series of strokes that, among other things, limited the use of his right hand.

Fortunately, Francis was not concerned with Leonardo's productivity. He enjoyed their conversations together and was honored to think that one of the most accomplished men in Europe was content to be his guest.

Leonardo soon turned his attention to organizing his notebooks. This was perhaps because of a renewed sense that they ought to be published. Here was the record of the wide variety of his life's work—notes and papers on everything from painting, bird flight, and the science of hydraulics to studies of animals, the bones and muscles of the human body, and the workings of the eye. Unfortunately, all of Leonardo's efforts were in vain—the notebooks were never published in his lifetime.

Before long, the little energy Leonardo had left was consumed by the simple tasks of getting through each day. In his dying months, according to Vasari, Leonardo "set himself to study the holy Christian religion, and though he could not stand, desired to leave his bed with the help of his friends and servants to receive the Holy Sacrament."

Francesco Melzi

Leonardo wrote his will on April 23, 1519, knowing he had little time left. Most of his art and notebooks he left to his former student and current companion, Francesco Melzi, who had served him for many years. Leonardo also left instructions for an elaborate funeral.

Sketching animals, such as cats and lions, engaged in the typical activities that would fill their days, was useful practice for Leonardo in case he decided to put them in a painting.

When designing experiments, Leonardo first drew the apparatus required. Seeing the different pieces laid out on the page helped him to imagine how the experiment would work.

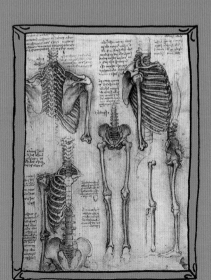

Drawing the different bones in the human body and understanding how they fit together was very important to Leonardo as he prepared to depict people in various poses.

"While **I** thought that I was **learning** how to **live,** I have **been learning** how to *die.*"

Leonardo,
from his private
notebooks

His time in this world might be up, but he had always prided himself on making a memorable impression. He had no intention of quietly fading away without an extremely grand send-off. Whatever else people might say about him after he was gone, they would remember that he had made his departure in style.

Since Leonardo was no longer up and about, it had become King Francis's habit to visit him regularly. At this late date, Leonardo spoke of how "he had offended God and men by not working at his art" as diligently as he might have. But there was little remaining time for regrets.

On May 2, Vasari stated that as Leonardo was suffering, "the king raised him and lifted his head to help him and lessen the pain, whereupon his spirit, knowing it could have no greater honor, passed away in the king's arms ..."

The dying Leonardo is held by Francis I in this imaginary scene painted in 1818 by the French artist Jean-Auguste-Dominique Ingres.

A true **Renaissance Man**

With a thirst for knowledge and understanding that could never be quenched, Leonardo truly embodied the spirit of the Renaissance.

Just as Leonardo's life was filled with travel and adventure, his restless mind never stayed put in one place for long—it was always seeking out new challenges. He came up with more ideas in his 67 years than he had time to properly address.

Clearly, he took advantage of the support offered to artists and thinkers in the 1400s and 1500s. His unique combination of talents earned him attention and fame across Europe.

"The loss of Leonardo," wrote Vasari, "was mourned out of measure by all who had known him, for there was none who had done such honor to painting."

This red-chalk drawing is thought to be a self-portrait of Leonardo.

"The splendor of his **great beauty** could calm the saddest soul, and his words could **move the most obdurate mind.**"

Giorgio Vasari,
The Lives of the Most Excellent Painters, Sculptors, and Architects,
1550

But Leonardo was distinguished by more than just his artistic and technical skills. As Vasari explained, "His great strength could restrain the most violent fury, and he could bend an iron knocker or a horseshoe as if it were lead." His personal warmth also set him apart. "He was liberal to his friends, rich and poor, if they had talent and worth; and indeed as Florence had the greatest of gifts in his birth, so she suffered an infinite loss in his death."

The reality of that loss showed how highly Leonardo had been regarded during his own life. Yet Leonardo was a man far ahead of his time as well. Among his many ideas that would become realities hundreds of years later were the tank, the helicopter, the bicycle, and the submarine. He devised levers and cranes and screws that could perform in ways never thought of before.

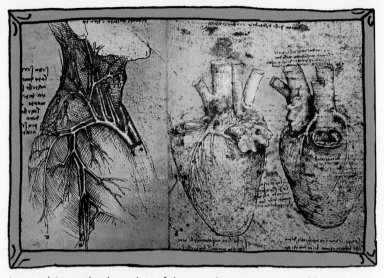

Leonardo's notebook studies of the circulatory system and heart

As a painter, Leonardo had few rivals, and he was alone in his devotion to seeing things below the surface. Leonardo was never satisfied to just copy what he saw with his eyes. To reproduce an image properly, he had to understand everything about it. So if he was drawing the human body, he had to understand precisely how the muscles and joints came together.

Leonardo's investigations into the workings of the human body led him far beyond the frontiers of Renaissance medicine. His notebooks were filled with unique observations on the skeleton, the digestive system, the brain, and the heart.

Such discoveries could have revolutionized medical science at the time. However, none were published, either during Leonardo's life or for centuries after his death. This greatly limited their influence, but they remain amazing achievements.

For such a famous artist, it may seem odd that Leonardo completed only a handful of paintings. Some of his reluctance to finish projects came from having a curious mind that was almost too eager to embrace new things.

This statue of Leonardo was sculpted by Luigi Pampaloni in the 1800s. It is in the courtyard of the Uffizi Gallery, Florence.

However, once his mind was engaged in a task, he would not be hurried. He was committed to the most exhaustive examinations of whatever topic currently obsessed him. To do that properly took time and effort—it would not happen by accident. "Develop your senses—especially learn how to see," he declared. "Realize that everything connects to everything else."

Leonardo was ambitious and proud of his accomplishments, but he did not take himself so seriously that he couldn't also make fun of himself. "The worst evil which can befall the artist," Leonardo noted with some amusement, "is that his work should appear good in his own eyes."

He never stopped searching for lofty goals, and when he achieved one, he was satisfied only until a new challenge came along.

Leonardo's tomb is in the Chapel of St. Hubert at Château d'Amboise. The remains in the tomb are thought to be Leonardo's, but no one knows for sure.

In the end, he stood, and continues to stand, at that place where art and science meet. Like the Vitruvian Man he once drew, Leonardo achieved a measure of balance and proportion in his life that was rare in his own time—and has remained rare ever since.

109

Leonardo's
family tree

Antonio da Vinci
c.1372–1468

Grandfather

Lucia
c.1393–1469

Grandmother

Albiera di Giovanni Amadori
1436–1464

Stepmother

Ser Piero da Vinci
1427–1504

Father

Leonardo da Vinci
1452–1519

Caterina was a peasant.

Mother

Caterina di Meo Lippi
unknown

Stepfather

Antonio Buti
unknown

Antonio made his living by making lime.

Timeline

The Peace of Lodi is signed, which will last 40 years, ensuring that Leonardo's childhood is without war.

Leonardo da Vinci is born in Anchiano, Italy, on April 15.

Leonardo receives a major commission for a painting of the Three Kings meeting the baby Jesus—the *Adoration of the Magi*.

1452   **1454**   **1466**   **1473**   **1481**

Leonardo goes to work as an artist's apprentice for Andrea del Verrocchio.

Leonardo draws *Arno Valley Landscape*, a pen-and-ink drawing that is the first work attributed to him as an artist.

The French invade Milan. The bronze metal Leonardo was going to use for his sculpture of Francesco Sforza is used for cannons instead.

Around this time, Leonardo draws *The Virgin and Child with St. Anne and St. John the Baptist.*

Leonardo draws the Vitruvian Man in one of his notebooks.

1482

1490

1495-98

1499

1500

Leonardo works on *The Last Supper* mural, a commission from the friars at a church in Milan.

Leonardo leaves Milan, eventually returning to Florence.

Leonardo travels to Milan to work as a military engineer for the Sforza family.

At 24 years old, Michelangelo, who did not get along with Leonardo, finishes his sculpture *Pietà*.

The leaders of Florence send Leonardo and Niccolò Machiavelli to negotiate with Cesare Borgia and avoid invasion. Leonardo begins working with Borgia as a military engineer.

Leonardo is asked to return to Milan.

Leonardo moves to Rome.

1502 1503 1504 1506 1513 1515

Ser Piero, Leonardo's father, dies.

Leonardo completes his last major painting, *St. John the Baptist*.

Leonardo begins painting the *Mona Lisa*, which he will work on for around 16 years.

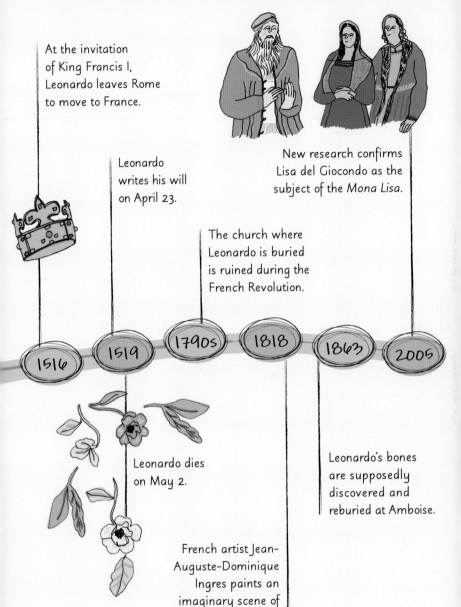

At the invitation of King Francis I, Leonardo leaves Rome to move to France.

Leonardo writes his will on April 23.

New research confirms Lisa del Giocondo as the subject of the *Mona Lisa*.

The church where Leonardo is buried is ruined during the French Revolution.

1516   1519   1790s   1818   1863   2005

Leonardo dies on May 2.

Leonardo's bones are supposedly discovered and reburied at Amboise.

French artist Jean-Auguste-Dominique Ingres paints an imaginary scene of Leonardo dying in King Francis's arms.

Quiz

1. When Leonardo da Vinci was born, Italy was not yet a country. What was it?

2. What kind of animal fossil did young Leonardo find in a cave?

3. How old was Leonardo when he became an apprentice to Andrea del Verrocchio?

4. Why did Leonardo buy caged birds?

5. What is the name of the famous mural Leonardo painted for the friars at the Church of Santa Maria delle Grazie in Milan?

6. Why did Leonardo write from right to left?

7. What did the French army do to Leonardo's clay statue of a horse in Milan?

**Do you remember what you've read?
How many of these questions about
Leonardo's life can you answer?**

 Who did Florence send along with Leonardo to negotiate with Cesare Borgia?

 How long did Leonardo work on the *Mona Lisa*?

 What is the name of Leonardo's last major painting?

 How long did it take Leonardo to make the 900-mile (1,500-km) journey from Rome, Italy to Amboise, France?

 What happened to the church where Leonardo was buried?

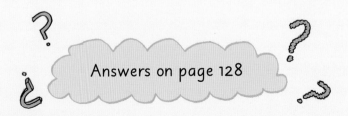

Answers on page 128

Who's who?

Alexander VI
(1431–1503) pope from
1492 to 1503

Bayezid II
(1447/48–1512) sultan of
the Ottoman Empire from
1481 to 1512

Borgia, Cesare
(1475/76–1507) military
leader and illegitimate son
of Pope Alexander VI

Botticelli, Sandro
(1445–1510) Italian
Renaissance artist who
painted *Primavera* (*Spring*)

**Buonarroti,
Michelangelo**
(1475–1564) Italian artist
and architect whose famous
works include the ceiling of
the Sistine Chapel, the *Pietà*,
and *David*

Charles VIII
(1470–1498) king of France
from 1483 to 1498; invaded
Italy in 1494

de Medici, Cosimo
(1389–1464) banker whose
family ruled Florence

**de Medici, Giulio
di Giuliano**
(1478–1534) Lorenzo
de Medici's nephew,
Leo X's cousin

de Medici, Lorenzo
(1449–1492) Leonardo's
patron, grandson of
Cosimo de Medici

**del Giocondo,
Francesco**
(1465–1538) merchant who
commissioned Leonardo to
paint a portrait of his wife,
Lisa Gherardini (*Mona Lisa*)

del Verrocchio, Andrea
(1435–1488) Italian artist
who Leonardo worked
under as an apprentice

Francis I
(1494–1547) king of
France from 1515 to
1547; standardized
the French language

Gherardini, Lisa
(1479–1542) subject
of the *Mona Lisa*; wife of
Francesco del Giocondo

Ingres, Jean-Auguste-Dominique
(1780–1867) French artist
who painted a scene
showing Leonardo dying
in the arms of Francis I

Leo X
(1475–1521) pope from
1513 to 1521; Lorenzo de
Medici's son and Giuliano
de Medici's cousin

Louis XII
(1462–1515) king of
France from 1498 to 1515;
conquered Milan in 1499

Machiavelli, Niccolò
(1469–1527) Italian
politician and philosopher

Melzi, Francesco
(1491/93–1570)
Leonardo's student and
longtime companion

Pampaloni, Luigi
(1791–1847) Italian
sculptor who carved
a statue of Leonardo

Raphael (Raffaello Sanzio da Urbino)
(1483–1520) Italian artist
whose famous works include
The School of Athens

Rubens, Peter Paul
(1577–1640) Flemish
artist who drew a copy of
Leonardo's *Battle of Anghiari*

Sforza, Francesco
(1401–1466) father of
Ludovico Sforza and
duke of Milan from
1450 to 1466

Sforza, Ludovico
(1452–1508) duke of Milan
from 1494 to 1499

Vasari, Giorgio
(1511–1574) Italian painter,
writer, and architect; Vasari
wrote an account of
Leonardo's life

Venusti, Marcello
(c.1512–1579) Italian artist
who probably painted
Crucifixion in 1540

Vitruvius
(1st century BCE) ancient
Roman architect whose
work inspired Leonardo

Glossary

air-screw
spinning device, like a propeller or helicopter blade, that enables an aircraft to fly

apparatus
tool or machine made for a specific job

apprentice
young student who learns a trade from a master

bilge pump
machine that removes sewage or extracts unwanted water from places

campaign
series of military actions during a war

caravan
group of travelers

city-state
an independent state made up of a city and the land around it

commission
money given to an artist in exchange for future work

crucifixion
execution by nailing or binding a person to a cross

disciple
follower

distinctive
special

eclipsed
made less important

emerge
to come out of

estate
property and wealth left by a person on their death

fleur-de-lis
traditional symbol of the French monarchy, a golden lily on a blue background

flourish
to be successful

fossil
remains of a prehistoric animal or plant preserved in rock

fresco
wall painting created on wet plaster

frontier
border between two places or things

gentleman
man born into a family of high social standing

gristmill
machine that grinds cereal grains into a powder that can be used to make bread

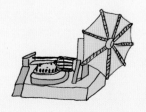

grove
small area with trees

Holy Sacrament
bread and wine taken by Christians in remembrance of the Last Supper of Jesus and his followers

horizon line
where land and sky meet

hydraulics
science that studies the power of moving liquids

illegitimate
not recognized by law

lime
substance made by heating limestone or shells, used in mortar, plaster, and pottery

lofty
high in status

Magi
in the Bible, kings, or
wise men who visited
the baby Jesus

majestic
grand

masonry bridge
bridge supported by a
foundation of brick or stone
held together with mortar

master
someone who is very
good at their trade

mirror writing
backward writing that can
only be read by holding it
up to a mirror

monastery
place where monks live,
work, and worship

mural
wall painting

negotiator
someone who discusses
problems with others in
order to find a solution

notary
public official who
helps people create legal
documents and contracts

obdurate
stubborn

patron
wealthy lord or merchant
who gives money to an artist

peasant
poor person who worked
on the land growing crops

pedestal
base for a statue

perspective
how things look when they
are closer or farther away

pondered
thought about seriously

pope
head of the Catholic
Church, based in Rome

prior
Christian person overseeing
a church or religious house

profile
side view of a head or face

propinquity
closeness

proportion
relationship of part
to whole

Renaissance
time of great advances in
European civilization, which
began around 1300

renovated
restored to a better condition

retainer
steady salary

sfumato
painting technique in which
tones and colors are slowly
blended together

splendor
magnificence

sultan
Islamic ruler

suspension bridge
bridge supported by cables
hanging from towers at
either end of the bridge

tempera
water-and-egg-based paint

toil
to work hard

transparent
see-through

unique
special

vanishing point
place in a painting or
drawing where different
sightlines meet

vineyard
place where grapevines
are planted

Index

Acknowledgments

The author would like to thank: Leslie Primo for his help in making sure that Leonardo would approve of what was written about him here.

DK would like to thank: Jacqueline Hornberger for proofreading; Hilary Bird for the index; Cécile Landau, Seeta Parmar, and Margaret Parrish for editorial help; Simran Lakhiani for additional design support; and Maya Frank-Levine for writing the reference section.

The publisher would like to thank the following for their kind permission to reproduce their photographs: (Key: a-above; b-below/bottom; c-center; f-far; l-left; r-right; t-top)

8 Alamy Stock Photo: imageBROKER / Martin Engelmann (b). 11 Dreamstime.com: Miunicaneurona (br). 15 Getty Images: Hulton Fine Art Collection / Imagno (cb). 22 Getty Images: Hulton Archive / Imagno (br). 23 Alamy Stock Photo: Cola Images (tr). 26 Getty Images: Corbis Historical / Leemage (b). 27 Alamy Stock Photo: classicpaintings (b). 29 Alamy Stock Photo: Ian Dagnall. 30–31 Dreamstime.com: Rudi1976 (b). 32 Alamy Stock Photo: World History Archive (tr). 35 Alamy Stock Photo: Photo 12 / Archives Snark (cr). Getty Images: Hulton Fine Art Collection / Print Collector (tl); Hulton Archive / Print Collector (bl). 36 Alamy Stock Photo: Art Collection 2 (clb). 37 Alamy Stock Photo: IanDagnall Computing. 40 Alamy Stock Photo: Art Collection 2 (clb). 41 Getty Images: Hulton Fine Art Collection / Heritage Images (t). 43 Alamy Stock Photo: Artepics (crb). 44–45 Alamy Stock Photo: PAINTING. 49 Depositphotos Inc: janaka (tr). 50 Getty Images: Universal Images Group / Universal History Archive (bl). 51 Alamy Stock Photo: Granger Historical Picture Archive / Granger, NYC. (cr); Historical Images Archive (tl); incamerastock / ICP (bl). 52 Dreamstime.com: Viktor Gladkov (crb). 53 Getty Images: Leonardo da Vinci (tr). 55 Alamy Stock Photo: Granger Historical Picture Archive / Granger, NYC. (tr). 57 Alamy Stock Photo: Boris Karpinski (clb). Getty Images: Hulton Fine Art Collection / Heritage Images (tr). 59 Alamy Stock Photo: Diana Bier Florence (t). 60 Alamy Stock Photo: Lebrecht Music & Arts. 62 Getty Images: Hulton Fine Art Collection / Mondadori Portfolio (clb). 63 Alamy Stock Photo: Everett Collection Historical (tc). 64 Alamy Stock Photo: GL Archive (tl). 65 Getty Images: Corbis Historical / Fratelli Alinari IDEA S.p.A. (t). 66 Getty Images: Hulton Fine Art Collection / Heritage Images (cla). 73 Alamy Stock Photo: Ian Dagnall. 75 Getty Images: Hulton Fine Art Collection / GraphicaArtis (tr). 76 Getty Images: Corbis Historical / Fine Art (b). 78 Alamy Stock Photo: Sorin Colac (bl). 80 Alamy Stock Photo: Artepics (t). 82 Alamy Stock Photo: classicpaintings (cr). 82–83 Getty Images: Moment / Alexander Spatari (b). 86 Dreamstime.com: Juliane Jacobs (clb). 87 Alamy Stock Photo: North Wind Picture Archives (cla); World History Archive (cb). 89 Getty Images: De Agostini / DEA / J. E. BULLOZ. 90 Getty Images: Hulton Archive / Heritage Images (clb). 91 Alamy Stock Photo: age fotostock / José Antonio Moreno (b). 94 Alamy Stock Photo: The Picture Art Collection (clb). 95 Alamy Stock Photo: ART Collection (tl); Dennis Hallinan (bl). Getty Images: Science & Society Picture Library (cr). 98–99 Alamy Stock Photo: Heritage Image Partnership Ltd / © Fine Art Images. 101 Alamy Stock Photo: The Picture Art Collection. 104 Alamy Stock Photo: Prisma Archivo (t). 105 Dreamstime.com: William Perry (bl). 107 Alamy Stock Photo: Vlad Ghiea. 109 Alamy Stock Photo: North Wind Picture Archives. 111 Getty Images: Corbis Historical / Stefano Bianchetti (bl)

Cover images: Front: Alamy Stock Photo: Science History Images / Photo Researchers b; Spine: Alamy Stock Photo: Science History Images / Photo Researchers ca

All other images © Dorling Kindersley
For further information see: www.dkimages.com

ANSWERS TO THE QUIZ ON PAGES 116—117

1. a group of city-states; 2. whale; 3. 14; 4. to set them free; 5. *The Last Supper*; 6. to avoid smearing the ink with his left hand; 7. used it for target practice; 8. Niccolò Machiavelli; 9. around 16 years; 10. *St. John the Baptist*; 11. about three months; 12. it was ruined during the French Revolution